Contents:

I0490847

1. Introduction
   - The shift to hybrid workplaces
   - Challenges of managing hybrid teams
   - The importance of team building in a hybrid workplace
2. Understanding Hybrid Workplaces
   - Definition and types of hybrid workplaces
   - Benefits of hybrid workplaces
   - Challenges in a hybrid workplace, including communication, collaboration, and team cohesion
3. The Importance of Team Building in a Hybrid Workplace
   - Trust, communication, and shared sense of purpose
   - Preventing silos and ensuring remote employees feel included and valued
   - Fostering camaraderie and employee morale
   - Enhancing team performance
4. Team Building Strategies for Hybrid Workplaces
   - Establishing clear communication channels and norms
   - Fostering an inclusive culture
   - Encouraging collaboration and knowledge sharing
   - Implementing regular check-ins and feedback sessions
   - Organizing a mix of virtual, in-person, and blended team-building activities
5. Virtual Team Building Activities
   - The importance of engaging remote employees
   - Popular virtual activities
     - Virtual escape rooms
     - Online trivia and quiz games
     - Remote team lunches or coffee breaks
     - Virtual book clubs or learning sessions
     - Online team-building games (e.g., Werewolf, Codenames)
   - Tips for successful virtual team-building events
6. In-Person Team Building Activities
   - Strengthening relationships among in-office employees
   - Examples of in-person activities
     - Team workshops and problem-solving exercises
     - Outdoor team-building events (e.g., ropes courses, scavenger hunts)
     - Social events (e.g., team lunches, happy hours, volunteer activities)
     - Icebreaker games and activities
   - Best practices for in-person team-building activities
7. Blended Team Building Activities
   - Bridging the gap between remote and in-office employees
   - Examples of blended activities
     - Hybrid brainstorming sessions, using video conferencing and collaborative tools
     - Shared learning experiences, such as webinars or online courses
     - Joint team celebrations, such as virtual holiday parties or milestone events
     - Collaborative projects that involve both remote and in-office employees
     - Simultaneous in-person and virtual team-building activities, using video conferencing and other digital tools
   - Tips for successful blended team-building events
8. Creating a Supportive and Inclusive Environment
   - Promoting a sense of belonging for all team members
   - Addressing unconscious biases
   - Encouraging open communication and feedback
   - Celebrating diversity and individual strengths

Team Building in a Hybrid Workplace:
Strengthening Connections and Enhancing Performance

9. Measuring the Impact of Team Building
   - The importance of evaluating team-building efforts
   - Methods for assessing the impact of team building
     - Employee surveys
     - Performance metrics
     - Observations of team interactions
     - Feedback from team members and managers
   - Adapting team-building strategies based on evaluation results
10. Case Studies of Successful Team Building in Hybrid Workplaces
    - Examples of organizations that have effectively implemented team-building initiatives in a hybrid environment
    - Lessons learned and best practices from these case studies
11. Future Trends in Team Building and Hybrid Workplaces
    - The evolving nature of work and the workplace
    - How technology is transforming team building and collaboration
    - The potential impact of virtual and augmented reality on team-building activities
    - The role of artificial intelligence in fostering team cohesion and collaboration
    - The importance of continuous learning and adaptability in the future of work
12. Conclusion
    - The significance of team building in a hybrid workplace
    - The role of HR professionals and managers in fostering a cohesive, engaged, and high-performing workforce
    - The need for continuous evaluation and adaptation of team-building strategies
    - Embracing the opportunities presented by the hybrid workplace to enhance team performance and organizational competitiveness

Chapter 1: Introduction

The modern workplace has undergone a significant transformation in recent years, driven by technological advancements, shifting societal norms, and unforeseen events such as the COVID-19 pandemic. One of the most notable changes has been the shift towards hybrid workplaces, which combine the flexibility of remote work with the traditional in-office environment. The rise of hybrid work has been accelerated by the widespread adoption of remote work during the pandemic, with many organizations recognizing the benefits of this new working model. According to a 2020 Gartner study, 82% of company leaders plan to allow employees to work remotely at least some of the time, even after the pandemic (Gartner, 2020).

In this new era of hybrid work, HR professionals and managers face the challenge of managing diverse teams that are often physically separated, with employees working from home, co-working spaces, or the office. This shift has necessitated a re-evaluation of traditional team-building approaches to ensure that all employees feel connected, valued, and engaged, regardless of their physical location.

The importance of team building in a hybrid workplace cannot be overstated. Research has long established the connection between team cohesion, employee engagement, and overall performance (Tuckman, 1965). In a hybrid workplace, fostering a sense of unity and belonging is even more critical to prevent the formation of silos and ensure that remote employees do not feel isolated or disconnected from their in-office colleagues (Grenny & Maxfield, 2017).

A case in point is Microsoft, which shifted to a hybrid work model during the pandemic and has since made a conscious effort to invest in team-building initiatives that cater to both remote and in-office employees. The company introduced a range of virtual team-building activities, including online workshops, trivia sessions, and virtual coffee breaks to foster a sense of connection and camaraderie among its dispersed workforce (Microsoft, 2020).

Similarly, another example of a successful team-building initiative in a hybrid work environment is Cisco. The company implemented regular check-ins and feedback sessions to ensure that all employees feel heard and valued, irrespective of their work location. Cisco also organized a mix of virtual, in-person, and blended team-building activities to create an inclusive and connected environment for all team members (Cisco, 2020).

In this booklet, we will delve into the world of team building in a hybrid workplace, providing insights and practical strategies to bridge the gap between remote and in-office employees and enhance overall team performance. We will explore the unique challenges and opportunities presented by hybrid work, and discuss how HR professionals and managers can adapt their team-building approaches to cater to the needs of a diverse and geographically dispersed workforce.

By exploring this topic, we aim to provide a comprehensive guide for HR professionals and managers who seek to foster a cohesive, engaged, and high-performing workforce in a hybrid workplace.

In summary, the introduction chapter sets the stage for understanding the importance of team building in a hybrid workplace, highlighting the unique challenges and opportunities that arise from managing diverse and geographically dispersed teams. By drawing on relevant research, real-world examples, and case studies, this booklet will provide HR professionals and managers with practical strategies and insights for fostering a cohesive, engaged, and high-performing workforce in the rapidly evolving world of hybrid work.

Chapter 2: Understanding Hybrid Workplaces

The emergence of hybrid workplaces has presented both opportunities and challenges for organizations. In this chapter, we will explore the concept of hybrid workplaces, their benefits, and the potential difficulties that HR professionals and managers may encounter in managing hybrid teams.

2.1 Definition and Types of Hybrid Workplaces

A hybrid workplace is a flexible working model that combines remote work and traditional in-office work, allowing employees to work from home, co-working spaces, or the office, depending on individual needs and preferences. This model has gained significant traction in recent years, driven by advancements in technology and shifting societal norms, and further accelerated by the COVID-19 pandemic (Gartner, 2020).

There are different types of hybrid workplace models, with varying degrees of flexibility. Some organizations may adopt a fully flexible approach, allowing employees to choose their work location based on their preferences and job responsibilities. Others may implement a more structured model, where employees are required to spend a predetermined number of days in the office each week or month. Some companies may opt for a role-based hybrid model, wherein certain roles are designated as remote or in-office based on the nature of the job (Forbes, 2021).

2.2 Benefits of Hybrid Workplaces

Hybrid workplaces offer several benefits to both employees and organizations:

1. *Increased Flexibility*: Hybrid work models provide employees with greater flexibility, allowing them to better balance their personal and professional lives. This can lead to higher job satisfaction, reduced stress, and improved work-life balance (Gallup, 2020).
2. *Enhanced Productivity*: Studies have shown that remote work can boost employee productivity by eliminating office distractions and reducing time spent on commuting (Stanford, 2020). In a hybrid workplace, employees can choose the work environment that best suits their productivity needs.
3. *Cost Savings*: Organizations can save on real estate and operational costs by reducing the physical office footprint and shifting to a more agile workplace (Global Workplace Analytics, 2020). Additionally, employees can save on commuting costs, which can contribute to their overall job satisfaction.
4. *Talent Attraction and Retention*: Hybrid work models can broaden the talent pool, enabling organizations to attract and retain top talent from diverse locations (LinkedIn, 2020). Employees, particularly those belonging to younger generations, increasingly value flexibility and may be more likely to stay with a company that offers a hybrid work model.

2.3 Challenges in a Hybrid Workplace

While hybrid workplaces offer numerous benefits, they also present challenges that must be addressed to ensure the success of this working model:

1. *Communication:* Managing communication in a hybrid workplace can be complex, as remote and in-office employees may have different access to information and communication channels. It is crucial for HR professionals and managers to establish clear communication protocols and invest in tools that facilitate seamless communication across the team.
2. *Collaboration:* Ensuring effective collaboration among remote and in-office employees can be challenging, as they may have different work schedules and availability. Organizations must adopt collaboration tools and practices that enable employees to work together effectively, regardless of their location.

3. *Team Cohesion:* Building and maintaining team cohesion in a hybrid workplace can be difficult, as remote employees may feel isolated from their in-office colleagues. It is essential for managers to create an inclusive environment and implement team-building strategies that cater to the needs of both remote and in-office employees.

A case study illustrating the successful implementation of a hybrid workplace model is Salesforce, a global technology company. Salesforce adopted a "Work from Anywhere" model in response to the pandemic, allowing employees to choose their preferred work location based on their role and preferences. The company provided employees with the necessary tools and resources to work effectively, regardless of their location, and implemented a range of virtual and in-person team-building activities to foster team cohesion and engagement (Salesforce, 2021).

In another example, Shopify, an e-commerce platform, transitioned to a "Digital by Default" model in 2020, allowing the majority of its employees to work remotely on a permanent basis. The company recognized the importance of maintaining a sense of connection among its dispersed workforce and implemented various team-building initiatives, such as virtual team lunches, online workshops, and collaboration sessions, to ensure that employees feel included and connected (Shopify, 2020).

Understanding the unique dynamics of hybrid workplaces is critical for HR professionals and managers seeking to build high-performance teams in this new working environment. By recognizing the benefits and challenges of hybrid work, organizations can develop strategies to address potential difficulties, such as communication, collaboration, and team cohesion, and leverage the opportunities presented by this flexible working model. In the following chapters, we will delve deeper into the importance of team building in a hybrid workplace and explore practical strategies and activities to strengthen connections and enhance team performance.

Chapter 3: The Importance of Team Building in a Hybrid Workplace

As organizations increasingly adopt hybrid work models, the importance of team building in this new context cannot be overstated. In this chapter, we will explore the significance of team building in a hybrid workplace and discuss its implications for employee engagement, collaboration, and overall team performance.

3.1 Fostering Team Cohesion and Trust

In a hybrid workplace, where employees are dispersed across various locations, fostering a sense of team cohesion and trust is more important than ever. Team cohesion is the degree to which team members feel connected to one another, share common goals, and support each other in achieving those goals (Carron et al., 1985). In a hybrid environment, HR professionals and managers must actively work to create a sense of unity and belonging among remote and in-office employees, to prevent the formation of silos and ensure that all team members feel valued and included.

Research has shown that high levels of trust and cohesion within teams are associated with increased job satisfaction, reduced turnover, and improved team performance (Costa, 2003). By investing in team-building activities that foster a sense of connection and trust among team members, organizations can reap the benefits of a more engaged, cohesive, and high-performing workforce.

3.2 Enhancing Collaboration and Communication

Effective collaboration and communication are vital for the success of any team, and this is especially true in a hybrid workplace. With employees working from different locations and on varying schedules, maintaining open and transparent communication channels can be challenging. Team-building activities can play a crucial role in enhancing collaboration and communication among team members, by providing opportunities for them to interact, share ideas, and develop a common understanding of the team's objectives and expectations.

A study conducted by MIT found that teams that engage in regular team-building activities are more effective in their communication and collaboration, leading to higher levels of performance and innovation (Pentland, 2012). By incorporating team-building activities into the hybrid work model, HR professionals and managers can help to bridge the communication gap and foster a collaborative and innovative work culture.

3.3 Boosting Employee Engagement and Job Satisfaction

Employee engagement and job satisfaction are critical factors that impact overall team performance and organizational success. In a hybrid workplace, remote employees may be at risk of feeling isolated or disconnected from their in-office colleagues, which can negatively affect their engagement levels and job satisfaction (Grenny & Maxfield, 2017).

Team-building activities that cater to the needs of both remote and in-office employees can help to foster a sense of connection and camaraderie, boosting employee engagement and satisfaction. A Gallup study found that employees who are engaged in their work are more likely to be productive, customer-focused, and profitable, and less likely to leave their organization (Harter et al., 2002). By investing in team-building initiatives, organizations can enhance employee engagement and satisfaction, leading to improved team performance and reduced turnover.

3.4 Strengthening Organizational Culture

Organizational culture is a powerful force that influences employee behavior, decision-making, and overall performance. In a hybrid workplace, maintaining a strong and cohesive organizational culture can be challenging, as remote and in-office employees may have different experiences and levels of connection to the organization.

Team-building activities can help to reinforce the organization's values, goals, and expectations, promoting a shared understanding and commitment among employees, regardless of their work location. A study by the Harvard Business Review found that companies with strong cultures outperformed their competitors in terms of customer satisfaction, revenue growth, and employee retention (Kotter & Heskett, 1992). By incorporating team-building activities that align with the organization's culture and values, HR professionals and managers can strengthen the organization's culture and enhance overall team performance.

Team building plays a critical role in the success of a hybrid workplace, as it fosters team cohesion and trust, enhances collaboration and communication, boosts employee engagement and job satisfaction, and strengthens organizational culture. By recognizing the unique challenges and opportunities presented by the hybrid work model, HR professionals and managers can develop and implement team-building activities that cater to the needs of both remote and in-office employees, ultimately creating a more connected, engaged, and high-performing workforce.

Chapter 4: Team Building Strategies for Hybrid Workplaces

In a hybrid workplace, building high-performance teams requires adopting effective strategies that cater to the needs of both remote and in-office employees. In this chapter, we will discuss five practical team-building strategies and provide examples and case studies to illustrate how these strategies can foster cohesion, collaboration, and engagement among team members in a hybrid work environment.

4.1 Establishing Clear Communication Channels and Norms

Clear communication channels and norms are essential for fostering a connected and collaborative hybrid workforce. HR professionals and managers should invest in communication tools that enable seamless interactions, such as Slack, Microsoft Teams, or Zoom. Additionally, they should establish guidelines on communication frequency, preferred channels, and response times to create a transparent and efficient communication environment.

Example: Automattic, the company behind WordPress, has developed a comprehensive communication system that includes the use of internal blogs called "P2s," which allow employees to share updates, ask questions, and provide feedback. This system ensures that all employees have access to the same information and can actively participate in discussions, regardless of their location (Automattic, 2021).

4.2 Fostering an Inclusive Culture

Creating an inclusive culture is vital for successful team building in a hybrid workplace. HR professionals and managers should actively promote diversity and inclusion by offering training programs, providing resources, and establishing policies that ensure equal opportunities for remote and in-office employees. This includes creating an environment where all team members feel valued, heard, and included.

Example: Salesforce, a leading customer relationship management software provider, has implemented several initiatives to foster an inclusive culture, such as its Employee Resource Groups (ERGs), which provide support, networking opportunities, and professional development resources to employees from diverse backgrounds (Salesforce, 2021).

4.3 Encouraging Collaboration and Knowledge Sharing

Promoting collaboration and knowledge sharing among team members is critical for building high-performance teams in a hybrid workplace. HR professionals and managers can facilitate this by organizing cross-functional projects, workshops, and "lunch-and-learn" sessions. These activities provide employees with opportunities to learn from one another, develop new skills, and build relationships across departments.

Example: Google has implemented a program called "g2g" (Googler-to-Googler), which encourages employees to share their knowledge and expertise with colleagues through informal training sessions, workshops, and presentations. This program fosters collaboration, knowledge sharing, and continuous learning among employees (Google, 2021).

4.4 Implementing Regular Check-Ins and Feedback Sessions

Regular check-ins and feedback sessions are crucial for maintaining employee engagement and addressing any challenges or concerns in a hybrid workplace. HR professionals and managers should schedule periodic one-on-one meetings, team huddles, and performance reviews to ensure that employees receive ongoing support and feedback, regardless of their work location.

Example: Adobe, a software company, has replaced its annual performance review process with a system called "Check-In," which encourages managers and employees to engage in regular, ongoing conversations about goals, performance, and development. This approach allows for more timely feedback and support, fostering stronger relationships and improved performance among team members (Adobe, 2021).

4.5 Organizing a Mix of Virtual, In-Person, and Blended Team-Building Activities

Organizing a combination of virtual, in-person, and blended team-building activities is essential for fostering connection and camaraderie among remote and in-office employees in a hybrid workplace. These activities can include virtual workshops, online games, in-person team outings, and offsite retreats, which provide opportunities for employees to connect, learn, and collaborate in various settings.

Example: HubSpot, a marketing software company, organizes a variety of team-building activities for its hybrid workforce, including virtual team lunches, online escape rooms, in-person team outings, and annual "HubSpot Connect" events, which bring remote and in-office employees together for a week of collaboration, learning, and fun. These activities help foster a sense of connection and camaraderie among team members, regardless of their work location (HubSpot, 2021).

Adopting effective team-building strategies in a hybrid workplace is essential for fostering cohesion, collaboration, and engagement among remote and in-office employees. By establishing clear communication channels and norms, fostering an inclusive culture, encouraging collaboration and knowledge sharing, implementing regular check-ins and feedback sessions, and organizing a mix of virtual, in-person, and blended team-building activities, HR professionals and managers can help their teams navigate the challenges and opportunities of the hybrid work model and achieve greater success.

Chapter 5: Virtual Team Building Activities

This chapter will discuss the importance of engaging remote employees, explore popular virtual team-building activities, and provide tips for successfully organizing and conducting these events.

5.1 The Importance of Engaging Remote Employees

Remote employees often face unique challenges, such as feelings of isolation, reduced opportunities for networking and collaboration, and difficulties in building strong relationships with their colleagues. By implementing virtual team-building activities, organizations can help remote employees feel more connected, engaged, and valued, ultimately leading to higher job satisfaction, improved performance, and a stronger organizational culture.

5.2 Popular Virtual Activities

A variety of virtual team-building activities can be tailored to meet the unique needs and preferences of remote employees. Some popular options include:

5.2.1 Virtual Escape Rooms

Virtual escape rooms are online versions of the popular team-building activity, where participants must work together to solve puzzles and unlock clues to "escape" a themed room. These activities promote problem-solving, collaboration, and communication skills among team members.

Example: Shopify, an e-commerce platform, has successfully implemented virtual escape rooms as a team-building activity for its remote employees. The company found that these events helped to break down barriers between team members and fostered a sense of connection and camaraderie (Shopify, 2021).

5.2.2 Online Trivia and Quiz Games

Online trivia and quiz games can be an engaging and entertaining way for remote employees to connect and compete in a fun, low-pressure environment. These activities can be customized to include a variety of topics, such as company history, industry-specific knowledge, or pop culture.

Example: Buffer, a social media management company, hosts regular online trivia nights for its remote workforce, providing an opportunity for employees to have fun, connect, and learn together (Buffer, 2021).

5.2.3 Remote Team Lunches or Coffee Breaks

Organizing virtual team lunches or coffee breaks can help remote employees build relationships and stay connected with their colleagues. These informal gatherings can be scheduled on a regular basis, providing an opportunity for team members to discuss work-related topics or simply catch up on personal news.

Example: Help Scout, a customer service software provider, hosts weekly "Café Talks," where remote employees join a video call to enjoy coffee or lunch together, fostering a sense of connection and belonging among team members (Help Scout, 2021).

5.2.4 Virtual Book Clubs or Learning Sessions

Virtual book clubs or learning sessions can encourage remote employees to share their knowledge, learn from one another, and engage in meaningful discussions on topics of interest. These events can be organized around a specific book, article, or training module and can provide a platform for employees to develop new skills and insights.

Example: Basecamp, a project management software company, runs a virtual book club where remote employees read and discuss books on topics such as leadership, productivity, and communication. This activity fosters learning, collaboration, and personal development among team members (Basecamp, 2021).

5.2.5 Online Team-Building Games

Online team-building games, such as Werewolf, Codenames, or other collaborative games, can help remote employees connect, collaborate, and have fun together. These games can be easily adapted for virtual play and can be an engaging way for employees to strengthen their relationships and teamwork skills.

Example: InVision, a digital product design platform, organizes regular online game nights for its remote workforce, providing an opportunity for employees to connect, have fun, and build relationships in a relaxed and enjoyable setting (InVision, 2021).

5.3 Tips for Successful Virtual Team-Building Events

To ensure the success of virtual team-building events, HR professionals and managers should consider the following tips:

1. Choose activities that are inclusive and accessible: Select activities that can accommodate employees with diverse interests, abilities, and time zones to ensure that all team members can participate and feel included.
2. Provide clear instructions and support: Make sure employees understand the objectives, rules, and technology requirements for each activity. Provide any necessary resources or training to ensure that all participants can fully engage in the event.
3. Encourage participation and engagement: Design activities that promote interaction and collaboration, and provide opportunities for employees to contribute their ideas, knowledge, and skills.
4. Schedule events during work hours: Whenever possible, organize virtual team-building activities during employees' regular working hours to respect their personal time and prevent burnout.
5. Gather feedback and iterate: After each event, collect feedback from participants to identify areas for improvement and to gauge the impact of the activity on employee engagement and satisfaction. Use this feedback to refine future events and ensure that they continue to meet the needs of your remote workforce.

Virtual team-building activities are essential for engaging remote employees in a hybrid workplace. By selecting inclusive and accessible activities, providing clear instructions and support, encouraging participation, scheduling events during work hours, and gathering feedback to improve future events, HR professionals and managers can help remote employees feel more connected, engaged, and valued, ultimately leading to a stronger and more resilient organization.

Chapter 6: In-Person Team Building Activities

This chapter will discuss the importance of in-person team-building activities, explore various examples of these activities, and provide best practices for planning and implementing them in a hybrid work environment.

6.1 Strengthening Relationships Among In-Office Employees

While remote employees face unique challenges in terms of engagement and connection, in-office employees can also benefit from team-building activities that promote collaboration, communication, and trust. By organizing in-person activities, HR professionals and managers can help in-office employees build stronger relationships with their colleagues, improving teamwork, morale, and overall performance.

6.2 Examples of In-Person Activities

There are various in-person team-building activities that can be tailored to meet the unique needs and preferences of in-office employees. Some popular options include:

6.2.1 Team Workshops and Problem-Solving Exercises

Team workshops and problem-solving exercises can help in-office employees develop their communication, collaboration, and critical thinking skills. These activities can involve working together to solve real-world problems, brainstorming solutions to hypothetical challenges, or participating in structured workshops designed to improve specific skill sets.

Example: Atlassian, a software development company, hosts regular "ShipIt Days," where employees work together in small teams to develop and present innovative solutions to company challenges. This activity fosters collaboration, creativity, and problem-solving skills among team members (Atlassian, 2021).

6.2.2 Outdoor Team-Building Events

Outdoor team-building events, such as ropes courses, scavenger hunts, or team sports, can provide a fun, engaging, and physically active way for in-office employees to bond and develop teamwork skills.

Example: Zappos, an online shoe and clothing retailer, organizes an annual "Ropes Course Day" for its employees, promoting team building, communication, and trust through a series of challenging outdoor activities (Zappos, 2021).

6.2.3 Social Events

Social events, such as team lunches, happy hours, or volunteer activities, can help in-office employees connect on a personal level, fostering a sense of camaraderie and belonging.

Example: Salesforce, a cloud computing company, encourages its employees to participate in volunteer activities through its "Volunteer Time Off" program. By volunteering together, team members can strengthen their relationships while making a positive impact on their communities (Salesforce, 2021).

6.2.4 Icebreaker Games and Activities

Icebreaker games and activities can help in-office employees get to know each other better, build trust, and create a more inclusive and welcoming work environment.

Example: Google uses a variety of icebreaker games during its new employee orientation program, such as "Two Truths and a Lie" or "The Human Knot," to help newcomers feel more comfortable and connected with their colleagues (Google, 2021).

6.3 Best Practices for In-Person Team-Building Activities

To ensure the success of in-person team-building activities, HR professionals and managers should consider the following best practices:

1. Plan activities that cater to diverse interests and abilities: Choose activities that accommodate employees with different preferences, skills, and physical abilities to ensure that everyone can participate and feel included.
2. Set clear objectives and expectations: Clearly communicate the goals and desired outcomes of each activity, so employees understand the purpose and value of participating.
3. Encourage participation and inclusivity: Design activities that promote interaction and collaboration among all team members, and ensure that no one feels left out or excluded.
4. Be mindful of scheduling and time commitments: Plan activities during work hours, whenever possible, and consider the time constraints and availability of employees to ensure maximum participation and prevent burnout.
5. Evaluate and gather feedback: After each activity, collect feedback from participants to identify areas for improvement and assess the impact of the event on employee engagement, satisfaction, and team dynamics. Use this feedback to refine future activities and ensure they continue to meet the needs of your in-office workforce.
6. Create a balance between in-person and virtual activities: In a hybrid work environment, it's essential to strike a balance between in-person and virtual team-building events to engage both remote and in-office employees and foster a sense of unity and collaboration across the organization.

In-person team-building activities are essential for fostering strong relationships and a sense of camaraderie among in-office employees in a hybrid workplace. By selecting diverse and inclusive activities, setting clear objectives, encouraging participation, being mindful of scheduling, and gathering feedback for improvement, HR professionals and managers can create a more cohesive, engaged, and high-performing team.

Chapter 7: Blended Team Building Activities

Blended team-building activities play a vital role in bridging the gap between remote and in-office employees. These activities help create a sense of unity and collaboration among team members, regardless of their physical location. This chapter will discuss the importance of blended team-building activities, explore various examples of these activities, and provide tips for planning and implementing successful blended events in a hybrid work environment.

7.1 Bridging the Gap Between Remote and In-Office Employees

Blended team-building activities are essential for fostering a sense of unity and collaboration across the organization, ensuring that remote and in-office employees feel equally valued, engaged, and connected. By organizing blended activities, HR professionals and managers can help team members develop strong relationships, improve communication and collaboration, and create a more inclusive and high-performing work environment.

7.2 Examples of Blended Activities

There are various blended team-building activities that can be tailored to meet the unique needs and preferences of remote and in-office employees. Some popular options include:

7.2.1 Hybrid Brainstorming Sessions

Hybrid brainstorming sessions can involve using video conferencing and collaborative tools, such as shared whiteboards or documents, to encourage creative idea generation and problem-solving among both remote and in-office employees.

Example: IBM uses hybrid brainstorming sessions to generate innovative ideas and solutions, leveraging video conferencing and collaborative tools to facilitate seamless communication and collaboration among its global workforce (IBM, 2021).

7.2.2 Shared Learning Experiences

Shared learning experiences, such as webinars or online courses, can help remote and in-office employees develop new skills and knowledge together, fostering a sense of unity and shared purpose.

Example: Adobe offers a wide range of webinars, online courses, and workshops for its employees, providing opportunities for remote and in-office workers to learn and grow together (Adobe, 2021).

7.2.3 Joint Team Celebrations

Joint team celebrations, such as virtual holiday parties or milestone events, can help remote and in-office employees connect and celebrate achievements together, fostering a sense of camaraderie and belonging.

Example: Microsoft organizes joint virtual and in-person holiday parties, leveraging video conferencing and other digital tools to ensure that both remote and in-office employees can participate in the festivities (Microsoft, 2021).

7.2.4 Collaborative Projects

Collaborative projects that involve both remote and in-office employees can help promote teamwork, communication, and problem-solving skills across the organization.

Example: Slack, a communication platform provider, assigns cross-functional teams made up of remote and in-office employees to work on collaborative projects, fostering strong relationships and a sense of shared purpose (Slack, 2021).

7.2.5 Simultaneous In-Person and Virtual Team-Building Activities

Simultaneous in-person and virtual team-building activities can involve using video conferencing and other digital tools to facilitate interaction and engagement among both remote and in-office employees.

Example: Cisco, a technology company, hosts simultaneous in-person and virtual hackathons, allowing remote and in-office employees to collaborate and innovate together (Cisco, 2021).

7.3 Tips for Successful Blended Team-Building Events

To ensure the success of blended team-building events, HR professionals and managers should consider the following tips:

1. Choose activities that are inclusive and accessible: Select activities that can accommodate employees with diverse interests, abilities, and time zones to ensure that all team members can participate and feel included.
2. Leverage technology effectively: Use video conferencing, collaborative tools, and other digital platforms to facilitate seamless communication and interaction among remote and in-office employees.
3. Foster a sense of unity and shared purpose: Design activities that promote collaboration and teamwork, and emphasize the importance of working together towards common goals, regardless of employees' physical locations.
4. Be mindful of time zones and scheduling: When planning blended activities, consider the time zones of all participants and schedule events at times that are convenient for as many team members as possible.
5. Communicate expectations and goals clearly: Ensure that all participants understand the objectives and desired outcomes of each activity, so they can fully engage and contribute to the event's success.
6. Gather feedback and evaluate the impact: After each blended activity, collect feedback from participants to identify areas for improvement and assess the impact of the event on team dynamics, engagement, and satisfaction. Use this feedback to refine future activities and ensure they continue to meet the needs of your hybrid workforce.

Blended team-building activities are essential for fostering a sense of unity, collaboration, and engagement among remote and in-office employees in a hybrid work environment. By selecting inclusive and accessible activities, leveraging technology effectively, fostering a sense of shared purpose, and gathering feedback for continuous improvement, HR professionals and managers can create a more cohesive, engaged, and high-performing team in a hybrid workplace.

Chapter 8: Creating a Supportive and Inclusive Environment

It is crucial to create a supportive and inclusive environment for both remote and in-office employees to foster a sense of belonging, promote engagement, and ensure that all team members can contribute to their full potential. This chapter will discuss the importance of cultivating an inclusive environment, explore various strategies for promoting a sense of belonging, and provide practical tips for addressing unconscious biases, encouraging open communication, and celebrating diversity within hybrid teams.

8.1 Promoting a Sense of Belonging for All Team Members

Creating a supportive and inclusive environment starts with promoting a sense of belonging for all team members, regardless of their physical location. This involves acknowledging the unique challenges faced by remote and in-office employees, providing equitable opportunities for growth and development, and fostering a culture of empathy, respect, and understanding.

Research has shown that employees who feel a strong sense of belonging are more likely to be engaged, productive, and committed to their organizations (Gallup, 2020). Therefore, promoting a sense of belonging for all team members is essential for building high-performance teams in a hybrid work environment.

8.2 Addressing Unconscious Biases

Unconscious biases can negatively impact the experiences of remote and in-office employees, leading to disparities in opportunities, resources, and recognition. To create a supportive and inclusive environment, HR professionals and managers should be aware of their own unconscious biases and take proactive steps to address them. This may involve:

- Providing diversity and inclusion training for all employees
- Implementing blind recruitment processes to eliminate bias in hiring decisions
- Ensuring that performance evaluations are fair and consistent for both remote and in-office employees
- Actively seeking out diverse perspectives and opinions during team meetings and decision-making processes

Example: Google has implemented unconscious bias training for its employees, aiming to raise awareness of biases and provide strategies for addressing them in the workplace (Google, 2021).

8.3 Encouraging Open Communication and Feedback

Open communication and feedback are essential for fostering a supportive and inclusive environment in a hybrid workplace. By encouraging team members to share their thoughts, ideas, and concerns, HR professionals and managers can identify and address potential issues, promote collaboration, and ensure that all employees feel heard and valued.

Some strategies for encouraging open communication and feedback include:

- Implementing regular check-ins and feedback sessions for remote and in-office employees
- Providing multiple channels for communication, such as video calls, instant messaging, and team collaboration platforms
- Creating a psychologically safe environment where team members feel comfortable sharing their thoughts and opinions without fear of judgment or reprisal

Example: Salesforce has implemented a feedback culture that encourages employees to share their thoughts and ideas openly, fostering a sense of belonging and inclusivity for both remote and in-office workers (Salesforce, 2021).

8.4 Celebrating Diversity and Individual Strengths

Recognizing and celebrating the diverse backgrounds, skills, and strengths of remote and in-office employees is crucial for creating a supportive and inclusive environment. By acknowledging the unique contributions of each team member, HR professionals and managers can promote a sense of belonging, enhance collaboration, and foster a culture of mutual respect and appreciation.

Some strategies for celebrating diversity and individual strengths include:

- Implementing diversity and inclusion initiatives that promote awareness and appreciation of different cultures, backgrounds, and perspectives
- Recognizing and celebrating the unique skills and strengths of each team member, and leveraging those strengths to enhance team performance
- Organizing team-building activities that highlight the diverse talents and experiences of remote and in-office employees

Example: Atlassian has implemented a diversity and inclusion program called "Belonging at Atlassian," which aims to promote a sense of belonging for all employees by celebrating diversity, fostering inclusion, and providing opportunities for growth and development (Atlassian, 2021).

Creating a supportive and inclusive environment in a hybrid workplace is essential for fostering a sense of belonging, promoting engagement, and ensuring that all team members can contribute to their full potential. By addressing unconscious biases, encouraging open communication and feedback, and celebrating the diverse strengths of remote and in-office employees, HR professionals and managers can create a more cohesive, engaged, and high-performing team in a hybrid work environment.

Chapter 9: Measuring the Impact of Team Building

To ensure the effectiveness of team-building efforts in a hybrid workplace, it is essential for HR professionals and managers to evaluate the impact of these initiatives on team cohesion, engagement, and performance. This chapter will discuss the importance of assessing team-building efforts, explore various methods for evaluating their impact, and provide practical tips for adapting team-building strategies based on evaluation results.

9.1 The Importance of Evaluating Team-Building Efforts

Evaluating the impact of team-building efforts is critical for several reasons:

1. Assessing effectiveness: By measuring the impact of team-building activities, HR professionals and managers can determine whether these initiatives are achieving their desired outcomes, such as increased collaboration, improved communication, or enhanced team performance.
2. Identifying areas for improvement: Evaluating team-building efforts helps identify areas where further development or adjustments may be needed to ensure that these activities are meeting the needs of remote and in-office employees.
3. Ensuring return on investment: Team-building activities often require significant investments in terms of time, resources, and budget. Evaluating the impact of these efforts ensures that organizations are realizing a positive return on their investment.
4. Supporting continuous improvement: Regularly assessing the impact of team-building activities enables organizations to refine their strategies and make data-driven decisions that support continuous improvement and long-term success.

9.2 Methods for Assessing the Impact of Team Building

There are several methods for evaluating the impact of team-building efforts in a hybrid workplace:

1. Employee surveys: Conducting regular employee surveys can help organizations gather valuable insights into the effectiveness of their team-building initiatives. Surveys may include questions about employees' perceptions of team cohesion, communication, and collaboration, as well as their overall satisfaction with team-building activities.
   Example: Adobe uses employee engagement surveys to gauge the effectiveness of their team-building efforts and identify areas for improvement (Adobe, 2021).
2. Performance metrics: Tracking key performance indicators (KPIs) related to teamwork, collaboration, and productivity can help organizations assess the impact of their team-building efforts. Examples of relevant KPIs may include the number of successful team projects completed, the time taken to resolve team conflicts, or improvements in individual performance.
3. Observations of team interactions: HR professionals and managers can observe team interactions during meetings, projects, or team-building activities to assess the impact of these efforts on team dynamics, communication, and collaboration.
4. Feedback from team members and managers: Gathering feedback from team members and managers can provide valuable insights into the effectiveness of team-building activities and help identify areas for improvement. This feedback can be collected through informal discussions, formal feedback sessions, or anonymous channels.

9.3 Adapting Team-Building Strategies Based on Evaluation Results

After evaluating the impact of team-building efforts, HR professionals and managers should use the insights gained to adapt their strategies and improve the effectiveness of future team-building initiatives. This may involve:

1. Addressing identified gaps or areas for improvement: If the evaluation results indicate that specific aspects of team-building efforts are not meeting the needs of remote or in-office employees, HR professionals and managers should take steps to address these gaps and enhance the effectiveness of their initiatives.

2. Experimenting with new approaches: Based on the evaluation results, organizations may consider testing new team-building activities or approaches to better meet the needs of their hybrid workforce.

3. Focusing on high-impact activities: By identifying the team-building activities that have the most significant positive impact on team cohesion, engagement, and performance, organizations can allocate their resources more effectively and prioritize high-impact initiatives.

4. Continuously monitoring and evaluating team-building efforts: Regularly evaluating the impact of team-building activities ensures that organizations can continually refine their strategies and make data-driven decisions to support long-term success in a hybrid work environment.

Measuring the impact of team-building efforts is essential for ensuring the effectiveness and continuous improvement of these initiatives in a hybrid workplace. By employing various evaluation methods, such as employee surveys, performance metrics, observations of team interactions, and feedback from team members and managers, HR professionals and managers can gather valuable insights into the success of their team-building strategies. These insights can then be used to adapt and refine team-building activities, ensuring that they meet the needs of both remote and in-office employees and contribute to the overall success of the organization.

Chapter 10: Case Studies of Successful Team Building in Hybrid Workplaces

This chapter highlights several case studies of organizations that have successfully implemented team-building initiatives in a hybrid work environment. These examples provide valuable insights into the strategies, best practices, and lessons learned from organizations that have effectively fostered team cohesion, engagement, and performance in a hybrid workplace.

Case Study 1: Cisco Systems

Cisco Systems, a multinational technology company, has embraced a hybrid work model that incorporates both remote and in-office employees. The company has successfully implemented various team-building initiatives to ensure that its diverse workforce remains connected and engaged.

One of Cisco's team-building strategies is the use of Cisco Spark, a digital collaboration platform that enables employees to communicate and collaborate effectively, regardless of their location. The platform allows team members to chat, share files, and hold virtual meetings, fostering a sense of community and collaboration among remote and in-office employees (Cisco, 2021).

Additionally, Cisco hosts regular in-person team-building events, such as hackathons, workshops, and social gatherings, which provide opportunities for remote employees to visit the office and connect with their colleagues in person. The company also offers a flexible work environment, allowing employees to choose their preferred working arrangements, which further promotes a sense of belonging and connection among team members.

Key lessons and best practices from Cisco Systems:

- Leverage digital collaboration tools to facilitate communication and collaboration among remote and in-office employees.
- Offer flexible work arrangements to accommodate employees' diverse needs and preferences.
- Host regular in-person team-building events to strengthen connections among team members.

Case Study 2: Atlassian

Atlassian, an Australian software company, has adopted a hybrid work model and implemented various team-building initiatives to foster a sense of belonging and collaboration among its employees. The company emphasizes the importance of psychological safety and encourages open communication, feedback, and the sharing of ideas among team members (Atlassian, 2021).

One of Atlassian's team-building strategies is the use of "team playbooks," which are a collection of guidelines, best practices, and exercises designed to help teams improve collaboration, communication, and performance. These playbooks are regularly updated and adapted based on feedback from team members, ensuring that they remain relevant and effective in a hybrid work environment.

Atlassian also invests in regular team-building activities, both virtual and in-person, to help employees connect and build relationships. Examples of these activities include virtual coffee breaks, team lunches, and online games.

Key lessons and best practices from Atlassian:

- Foster psychological safety and encourage open communication and feedback among team members.
- Develop and maintain team playbooks to guide team collaboration and performance in a hybrid work environment.
- Organize regular virtual and in-person team-building activities to strengthen connections among employees.

Case Study 3: Siemens

Siemens, a multinational conglomerate, has adopted a hybrid work model and implemented various team-building initiatives to ensure that its employees remain connected and engaged. The company's "New Normal Working Model" allows employees to work remotely for two to three days per week, providing flexibility and accommodating diverse work preferences (Siemens, 2021).

One of Siemens' team-building strategies is the use of virtual collaboration tools, such as Microsoft Teams, which enable employees to communicate and collaborate effectively, regardless of their location. The company also offers a variety of team-building activities, including virtual workshops, online training sessions, and social events, to help employees connect and build relationships.

Additionally, Siemens provides resources and support for managers to help them effectively lead and engage their teams in a hybrid work environment. This includes training programs, guidelines, and best practices for managing remote and in-office employees.

Key lessons and best practices from Siemens:

- Offer flexible work arrangements to accommodate diverse work preferences and promote a sense of belonging among employees.
- Utilize virtual collaboration tools to facilitate communication and collaboration among team members.
- Provide a variety of team-building activities, both virtual and in-person, to help employees connect and build relationships.
- Offer resources and support for managers to effectively lead and engage their teams in a hybrid work environment.

These case studies demonstrate the importance of implementing effective team-building strategies in a hybrid work environment. The lessons and best practices from Cisco Systems, Atlassian, and Siemens showcase the value of leveraging digital collaboration tools, offering flexible work arrangements, fostering psychological safety, and investing in regular team-building activities to create a supportive and inclusive environment for remote and in-office employees.

By learning from these successful examples, HR professionals and managers can develop and implement their own team-building initiatives that cater to the unique needs and preferences of their workforce in a hybrid work environment, ensuring a strong sense of cohesion, engagement, and high performance among their teams.

Chapter 11: Future Trends in Team Building and Hybrid Workplaces

As the nature of work and the workplace continues to evolve, so too will the strategies and tools used for team building in hybrid environments. This chapter explores several future trends that are expected to shape the landscape of team building and collaboration in the coming years, including technological advancements, virtual and augmented reality, artificial intelligence, and the importance of continuous learning and adaptability in the future of work.

11.1 The Evolving Nature of Work and the Workplace

The traditional office environment has undergone significant transformation in recent years, with remote work becoming an increasingly common and accepted practice. As organizations adapt to these changes and embrace hybrid work models, team-building strategies will need to evolve accordingly, focusing on fostering connections among employees regardless of their location and supporting collaboration across both digital and physical spaces.

11.2 How Technology is Transforming Team Building and Collaboration

Technology has played a pivotal role in enabling remote work and collaboration, and its influence is expected to grow even more in the future. Digital collaboration tools, such as video conferencing, project management software, and instant messaging platforms, have become essential for facilitating communication and collaboration among remote and in-office employees. As these tools continue to improve and expand their capabilities, organizations will have even more opportunities to foster team cohesion and engagement in a hybrid work environment.

11.3 The Potential Impact of Virtual and Augmented Reality on Team-Building Activities

Virtual and augmented reality (VR and AR) technologies have the potential to revolutionize team-building activities in the future. These immersive technologies can create realistic, interactive experiences that enable employees to connect and collaborate in new and innovative ways, regardless of their physical location.

For example, virtual team-building activities could involve employees exploring a digital environment together, solving puzzles, or participating in team-based challenges, all while remaining physically remote. Augmented reality, on the other hand, could be used to overlay digital information and elements onto the physical world, allowing employees to interact with both real and virtual elements simultaneously.

As VR and AR technologies become more accessible and affordable, organizations will have new opportunities to create engaging and immersive team-building experiences that bridge the gap between remote and in-office employees.

11.4 The Role of Artificial Intelligence in Fostering Team Cohesion and Collaboration

Artificial intelligence (AI) is another technology that holds significant potential for shaping the future of team building and collaboration. AI-powered tools and platforms can analyze large amounts of data to identify patterns and trends, providing insights into team dynamics, communication, and performance.

For example, AI algorithms could be used to analyze team communication data and identify areas where collaboration is lacking, or to uncover potential conflicts or misunderstandings before they escalate. AI-powered tools could also be used to suggest personalized team-building activities or interventions based on individual and team preferences, strengths, and weaknesses.

As AI technology continues to advance, it will likely play an increasingly important role in helping organizations foster team cohesion, engagement, and high performance in a hybrid work environment.

11.5 The Importance of Continuous Learning and Adaptability in the Future of Work

As the nature of work continues to evolve, the importance of continuous learning and adaptability will only grow. Organizations and their employees will need to stay abreast of new developments, trends, and technologies that shape the future of work, and be prepared to adapt their team-building strategies accordingly.

This may involve investing in ongoing training and development for employees, as well as regularly re-evaluating and updating team-building initiatives to ensure they remain relevant and effective. By embracing a culture of continuous learning and adaptability, organizations can better navigate the changing landscape of work and ensure their teams remain cohesive, engaged, and high-performing, regardless of the challenges they face.

The future of team building in hybrid workplaces will likely be shaped by the ongoing evolution of work and the workplace, as well as the advancement and adoption of new technologies, such as virtual and augmented reality, artificial intelligence, and digital collaboration tools. These trends will create new opportunities and challenges for organizations as they strive to foster team cohesion, engagement, and high performance in an increasingly complex and dynamic work environment.

By staying informed about these trends and their potential impact on team building, HR professionals and managers can better prepare their organizations for the future of work. Embracing a culture of continuous learning and adaptability, along with leveraging the latest technology and tools, will be essential for organizations that want to thrive in the hybrid workplace and beyond.

12. Conclusion

The hybrid workplace, characterized by a combination of remote and in-office employees, has become increasingly prevalent in today's business landscape. As organizations navigate this new work environment, team building remains a crucial element in fostering a cohesive, engaged, and high-performing workforce. HR professionals and managers must recognize the significance of team building in a hybrid workplace and be prepared to implement innovative strategies to ensure the success of their teams.

Throughout this chapter, we have explored various aspects of team building in a hybrid workplace, including the importance of understanding the unique challenges and opportunities presented by such a work environment, as well as strategies and activities to promote collaboration, trust, and a sense of belonging among team members. Additionally, we have discussed the need for continuous evaluation and adaptation of team-building strategies to ensure their effectiveness in driving team performance and organizational competitiveness.

The role of HR professionals and managers in fostering a cohesive, engaged, and high-performing workforce in a hybrid workplace cannot be understated. They must take proactive steps to establish clear communication channels and norms, promote an inclusive culture, encourage collaboration and knowledge sharing, and organize a mix of virtual, in-person, and blended team-building activities. By doing so, they can help to bridge the gap between remote and in-office employees, and create a supportive environment in which all team members feel valued and empowered to contribute to their fullest potential.

Furthermore, HR professionals and managers must remain vigilant in their efforts to assess the impact of their team-building initiatives, using methods such as employee surveys, performance metrics, observations of team interactions, and feedback from team members and managers. This continuous evaluation process will enable organizations to identify areas for improvement and adapt their team-building strategies accordingly, ensuring that they remain effective in promoting team cohesion and high performance in the ever-evolving hybrid workplace.

Embracing the opportunities presented by the hybrid workplace requires organizations to adopt a forward-thinking and adaptable approach to team building. By leveraging the latest technology and tools, and fostering a culture of continuous learning and adaptability, organizations can not only enhance team performance but also position themselves for long-term success in an increasingly competitive business landscape.

In conclusion, team building in a hybrid workplace is an essential component of organizational success. HR professionals and managers must remain committed to fostering a cohesive, engaged, and high-performing workforce by implementing innovative team-building strategies, embracing new technology and tools, and continuously evaluating and adapting their approaches to team building. By doing so, they can harness the potential of the hybrid workplace to drive team performance and enhance their organization's competitiveness in today's dynamic business environment.

References:

Cisco. (2020). Building and Leading High-Performance Teams. Retrieved from
https://www.cisco.com/c/dam/en_us/training-events/events-webinars/webinars/conference/pdf/Building-and-Leading-High-Performance-Teams.pdf

Gartner . (2020). 9 Work Trends That Will Emerge in 2021. Retrieved from
https://www.gartner.com/smarterwithgartner/9-work-trends-that-will-emerge-in-2021/

Grenny, J., & Maxfield, D. (2017). A Study of Remote Workers. Retrieved from
https://www.vitalsmarts.com/press/2017/10/a-study-of-remote-workers/

Microsoft. (2020). The Future of Work: Building Resilience in a Hybrid Workplace. Retrieved from
https://www.microsoft.com/en-us/microsoft-365/blog/2020/10/08/the-future-of-work-building-resilience-in-a-hybrid-workplace/

Tuckman, B. W. (1965). Developmental sequence in small groups. Psychological Bulletin, 63(6), 384–399.
doi:10.1037/h0022100

Forbes. (2021). The Future of Hybrid Work: Three Models for Leaders to Consider. Retrieved from
https://www.forbes.com/sites/forbeshumanresourcescouncil/2021/03/25/the-future-of-hybrid-work-three-models-for-leaders-to-consider/?sh=14a61d2420d4

Gallup. (2020). How to Manage the New "Remote Work" Workforce. Retrieved from
https://www.gallup.com/workplace/283985/manage-new-remote-work-workforce.aspx

Global Workplace Analytics. (2020). Work-At-Home After COVID-19 – Our Forecast. Retrieved from
https://globalworkplaceanalytics.com/work-at-home-after-covid-19-our-forecast

LinkedIn. (2020). The Future of Recruiting: The Top 10 Recruiting Trends of 2021. Retrieved from
https://www.linkedin.com/pulse/top-10-recruiting-trends-2021-karsten-veddeler

Salesforce. (2021). The Future of Work is Here: Salesforce Adopts Work from Anywhere. Retrieved from
https://www.salesforce.com/news/stories/future-of-work/

Shopify. (2020). The Digital by Default Shopify: How We're Adapting to Thrive in a Post-COVID World. Retrieved from
https://www.shopify.com/blog/digital-by-default

Stanford. (2020). Does Working from Home Work? Evidence from a Chinese Experiment. Retrieved from
https://siepr.stanford.edu/research/publications/does-working-home-work-evidence-chinese-experiment

Carron, A. V., Brawley, L. R., & Widmeyer, W. N. (1985). The development of an instrument to assess cohesion in sport teams: The Group Environment Questionnaire. Journal of Sport Psychology, 7(3), 244-266.

Costa, A. C. (2003). Work team trust and effectiveness. Personnel Review, 32(5), 605-622.

Harter, J. K., Schmidt, F. L., & Hayes, T. L. (2002). Business-unit-level relationship between employee satisfaction, employee engagement, and business outcomes: a meta-analysis. Journal of Applied Psychology, 87(2), 268-279.

Kotter, J. P., & Heskett, J. L. (1992). Corporate Culture and Performance. Free Press.

Pentland, A. (2012). The New Science of Building Great Teams. Harvard Business Review. Retrieved from
https://hbr.org/2012/04/the-new-science-of-building-great-teams

Adobe. (2021). Adobe Check-In: A Continuous Performance Management Approach. Retrieved from
https://www.adobe.com/about-adobe/careers/check-in.html

Automattic. (2021). How We Stay Connected at Automattic. Retrieved from https://automattic.com/work-with-us/how-we-stay-connected/

Google. (2021). Googler-to-Googler: Peer-to-Peer Learning at Google. Retrieved from
https://www.google.com/about/careers/learning-and-development/

HubSpot. (2021). Building Connection in a Hybrid Work Environment. Retrieved from https://www.hubspot.com/careers-blog/building-connection-hybrid-work

Salesforce. (2021). Equality at Salesforce: Employee Resource Groups. Retrieved from
https://www.salesforce.com/company/equality/

Basecamp. (2021). Basecamp Book Club: Fostering Learning and Collaboration. Retrieved from
https://basecamp.com/books

Buffer. (2021). Buffer's Remote Team-Building Activities. Retrieved from https://buffer.com/resources/remote-team-building-activities/

Help Scout. (2021). Building Connection in a Remote Team: Help Scout's Café Talks. Retrieved from https://www.helpscout.com/blog/remote-team-building/

InVision. (2021). InVision's Remote Team Game Nights. Retrieved from https://www.invisionapp.com/inside-design/remote-team-building-activities/

Shopify. (2021). Shopify's Virtual Escape Room Experience. Retrieved from https://www.shopify.com/blog/remote-team-building

Atlassian. (2021). ShipIt Days: Fostering Innovation and Teamwork at Atlassian. Retrieved from https://www.atlassian.com/blog/inside-atlassian/shipit-days

Google. (2021). Google's New Employee Orientation: Icebreakers and Team Building. Retrieved from https://www.google.com/about/careers/lifeatgoogle/new-employee-orientation.html

Salesforce. (2021). Salesforce Volunteer Time Off: Building Teams Through Community Service. Retrieved from https://www.salesforce.com/company/careers/volunteer-time-off/

Zappos. (2021). Zappos Ropes Course Day: Team Building and Trust. Retrieved from https://www.zappos.com/c/ropes-course-day

Adobe. (2021). Adobe Learning and Development Programs. Retrieved from https://www.adobe.com/careers/learning-and-development.html

Cisco. (2021). Cisco Hackathon: Innovating Together in a Hybrid Work Environment. Retrieved from https://blogs.cisco.com/collaboration/cisco-hackathon-innovating-together

IBM. (2021). IBM Hybrid Brainstorming Sessions: Fostering Collaboration and Innovation. Retrieved from https://www.ibm.com/blogs/think/2021/08/ibm-hybrid-brainstorming-sessions/

Microsoft. (2021). Microsoft Joint Holiday Celebrations: Connecting Remote and In-Office Employees. Retrieved from https://www.microsoft.com/en-us/insidetrack/microsoft-joint-holiday-celebrations

Slack. (2021). Collaborative Projects at Slack: Fostering Teamwork and Innovation. Retrieved from https://slackhq.com/collaborative-projects-at-slack

Atlassian. (2021). Belonging at Atlassian. Retrieved from https://www.atlassian.com/belonging

Gallup. (2020). The Importance of Employee Belonging in the Workplace. Retrieved from https://www.gallup.com/workplace/325657/importance-employee-belonging-workplace.aspx

Google. (2021). Unconscious Bias Training at Google. Retrieved from https://diversity.google/programs/unconscious-bias-training/

Salesforce. (2021). Cultivating a Feedback Culture at Salesforce. Retrieved from https://www.salesforce.com/news/stories/cultivating-a-feedback-culture/

Adobe. (2021). Adobe Employee Engagement Surveys. Retrieved from https://www.adobe.com/corporate-responsibility/people/employee-engagement-surveys.html

Atlassian. (2021). Atlassian Team Playbooks. Retrieved from https://www.atlassian.com/team-playbook

Cisco. (2021). Cisco Spark. Retrieved from https://www.cisco.com/c/en/us/products/collaboration-spark/index.html

Siemens. (2021). New Normal Working Model. Retrieved from https://press.siemens.com/global/en/pressrelease/siemens-establishes-new-normal-working-model

Bersin, J. (2021). The Future of Work: The Intersection of Artificial Intelligence and Human Resources. Retrieved from https://joshbersin.com/2021/02/the-future-of-work-the-intersection-of-artificial-intelligence-and-human-resources/

Gartner. (2020). The Future of Work Reinvented: A Gartner Trend Insight Report. Retrieved from https://www.gartner.com/en/documents/3992298/the-future-of-work-reinvented-a-gartner-trend-insight-r

Kasriel, S. (2017). The Big Idea: Work, As We Knew It, Is Overrated. Here's a Better Way to Look at It. LinkedIn. Retrieved from https://www.linkedin.com/pulse/big-idea-work-we-knew-overrated-heres-better-way-look-stephane-kasriel

VirtualSpeech. (2021). The Ultimate Guide to Virtual Reality (VR) Team Building. Retrieved from https://virtualspeech.com/blog/virtual-reality-team-building

About the Author

Jude is a global workforce resourcing specialist, with lived experience leading large, remote, global, multi-cultural and outsourced teams. As a senior leader with a proven track record in delivering workforce management services, & implementing complex organisational transformation and change, Jude focuses on helping businesses design, review and implement their workforce frameworks to maximise value.

Through her previous experience in the global resources sector, Jude has championed, implemented and managed various cycles of in-house, outsource, centralise, decentralise, offshore, near-shore, remote, global and local service delivery strategies; and understands in-depth, what it takes to maintain success in any version of these workforce configurations.

A strong operational and customer service focus, passionate and skilled at people development and improving employee engagement, Jude is commercially astute and has managed budgets up to $18M. She is action-oriented, process driven and focused on sustainable business outcomes, with accreditations to deliver DISC, Workplace Motivators (Driving Forces), DNA and Emotional Intelligence psychometric assessments.

Available for advisory consulting, diagnostics & improvement projects, change & project management, operational delivery support and speaking engagements, Jude and her expert team of associates and partners can be deployed for short or long-term projects locally, nationally and internationally.

Find out more at JudeMahony.com or explore support options at OptimalResourcing.com.au

www.ingramcontent.com/pod-product-compliance
Lightning Source LLC
Chambersburg PA
CBHW071131220526
45467CB00004B/2130